Mating Season

Mating Season

poems by

Kate Gale

Tupelo Press

Dorset, Vermont

Mating Season

Copyright © 2004 by Kate Gale

ISBN 1-932195-17-3

Printed in Canada

Library of Congress Control Number:
2003115524
First paperback edition, 2004

Tupelo Press
PO Box 539, Dorset, Vermont 05261
802.366.8185   Fax 802.362.1883
editor@tupelopress.org   web www.tupelopress.org

Book design by Mark E. Cull
Cover Design by William Kuch, WK Graphic Design

for Mark

Contents

Mating Season

The Cemetery

I was the first child to swim out to the raft
in the crazy spring water.
The rest watched me from shore, wet to their ankles.
The water wasn't alive with leeches,
as it would be later, with heat
and us all growing out of our summer clothes.

Then the leeches would cling to your legs and back.
Up on the raft, you'd pick them off one by one,
knowing they'd be on you again and again
as you descended into the brackish water.
The air was tree sweet and in the shallows
rocks rose and pine needles floated.

The raft was makeshift and roped on oil drums.
We slipped underneath to talk secrets and peer at
people from below, their feet and their legs,
them padding around like so many penguins.
Later too, there would be frogs' eggs
and frogs croaking all night.

But that morning, it was liquid cold and very quiet.
There was the ticking of my first waterproof watch.
There was the sun not yet fully risen.
There were shadows huddling in the ankles of trees.
There was the cemetery looming over the pond,
those old gravestones.

I wondered if bodies or souls slid down into the oozing water,
the black decay I swam in.
The water was dreadful, eyes staring up from the bottom.
But I was growing, finally and that winter
I'd begun to cycle with the moon
so the water seemed no more terrible than that.

The girls on the shore watched
as I walked out dripping and we moved into the cemetery,
our fingers feeling gravestones for names.
The water in my shoes, sour and compressed. As we walked,
the air grew violent. A new snow was surely coming
and the gravestones would vanish until another thaw.

Winter breaks and closes all through
New England spring.

Crying in Front of a Man

To my first love, I wept profusely.
These tears confused the boy, and he would act.
Generally, he took me out to eat.
I grew fat, sobbing my way into some of the best
restaurants in Richmond.

My first husband ignored the initial shattering of tears.
But if I went on grovelling, wailing long enough
he'd collect me from the floor
give me a bit more grocery money, wipe my eyes
tell me it would be okay by and by.

My second husband despised my tears.
He'd seen women crawl and shake enough,
said the vipers can enter a trance at will
and let their sobs heave ho to twist a man
and bend him into shape.

I trouble not this third man with my tears.
Have in fact forgotten how to cry
and in forgetting have grown steel eyes,
a molten core like mad Vesuvius, am held in check
by nothing but the weather and the whims of fate.

Sunflowers

Wretched light coming in by the half open shutters.
Light saying get up. Daniel not moving.
Most days, Mother saying nothing.
Mouth full of cigarette, eyes full of alcohol,
Daniel's truancy of little matter.
Finally enrolled him as home school.
Most days he stared at the *Sunflowers*
above the bed. Climbed on a step ladder to touch.
Sunlight bruising the color until it faded.
An invitation to Van Gogh's country.

Early in the morning.
Running against the broad stairway.
Feels painfully slow. Rain against the windows.
Mother in a bathrobe with a coffee cup discovers the letter.
All running stops in the back of an ambulance.
Sirens and the woman's screams. Sirens get shut off.
She moans on like a rooster
who goes on announcing morning at midday.
Keening and moaning. But the running feet
are arrested. Questions asked. Explanations demanded.

Daniel drew a sketch of depression for the doctor.
Himself. Down a long deep hole.
Slowly filled with dirt.
Arrow with little words. Hole full of dirt.
Water seeps into hole here.
No air. No shovel.
Daniel went home clutching a bottle of pills.
With these, the doctor told him,
You'll be able to ignore the hole everybody falls into.
You'll be able to imagine yourself breathing and walking.

You'll walk around with a smile. Won't feel
like a misfit. Just be like everybody else.
That's what we want, don't we?
Rats. Daniel said. Rats.
Now let's stay rational, shall we?
Ah yes, Daniel said, Let's call these moments when we feel
soil in our mouth, fantasy, the moments when we're lumbering
along side by side with some cow with a fat lopsided smile
on our way to a burger and a sporting event,
let's call that socializing, the good life.

The doctor's smile plastered on like a clown's said,
Eat sarcasm. But he patted Daniel gently and said,
It's a long journey, but you're in good company.
Daniel remembered the grand staircase he'd ascended
so recently. The pills will slow the running feet.
He wants to climb the stairs into Van Gogh's *Sunflowers*,
the tips so thin and shaky.
He'll no longer be a danger to himself,
the doctor told his mother. In the ambulance
his mother's face very close to his,

looked yellow, the froth of her hair like petals.
For the last time, he let go of the edges.
Felt reality lift away like a loosening anchor chain.
His boat rocking gently on the shores of oblivion.
Surely all that was left wasn't eating dirt.
Learning to enjoy the taste.
Van Gogh, he says to himself at night.
Hears the yellow sunflowers whispering.
I'm all right, he tells them.
They haven't got me yet.

The Diggers

Andrew and John dug the soil back layer by layer.
To discover artifacts one must work carefully.
There is a skeleton with fistfuls of bright orange wig,
fluffed out around the grinning skull.
The molars are perfect. Some expensive dental work here.
The boss, Jésus keeps drinking his wine
won't pay attention. But the thing John likes
is the formed plastic over the ribcage,
one where each breast would be.
He tosses one to Andrew. These had to be fun.
Jésus has been drinking pretty steadily
since last weekend, probably won't stop
until he's done something foolish.
Last time he started a riot among the locals.
Andrew and John would like to finish their work
without disruption. There is gold hanging off the skeleton too.
They stop to eat fish tacos and celebrate the bag lady.
In the falling light, her bones shine white.
How those legs must have danced.
How that cleavage must have sparkled.
Jésus begins to howl. The brothers decide
to take him out for a pull around the lake.
The water quiets him. He slept through a storm once.
Then told the others he'd walked on water.
Like this skeleton he's crying after.
When he's done, she'll be his own dead wife.
Whoever she is, Jésus will claim her,
say that he died for her.
Ask that he be worshipped as a god.
Best to quiet him now.
Ever thought of drowning him? Andrew asks.
He's harmless, says John. Let's take him out
in the middle of the lake. Let him walk to shore.
With all that wine in him, not likely.

And what if those breasts were real, says Andrew.

Jésus is fast asleep now.

The boat is slipping along the waves like a lost dream.

Roll the Dice

Angry fellows on the road to Emmaus
pass by a couple disciples eating figs.
We saw Jesus, the fig eaters say.
Saw who? They kick some dirt up
so the dust settles on the disciples.
Here on the road, Jesus, the Messiah.
The angry men are looking for work.
One has an angry wife who said not to come back
without rent money.

Messiah for whom?
the married one asks.
The Jews, says one.
The whole world, says the other.
They're standing around in the road now;
it looks like rain.
Which way did your Messiah go?
says the first angry man.
Toward Jerusalem.

Let's play a game in the next tavern
the married man says.
We'll see if I'm a Messiah too.
If I am, you buy me dinner and wine.
If not, I'll buy yours.
Roll the dice, the disciple says, you're on.

Elizabeth

He's asleep on a rock when it starts. The girls rushing along like wings of barn swallows. He dives under brush, hears them stirring the air with their chat, whine, whistle, sing and did you know and did you hear and is it true, and I'm going in skinny dipping. What if you get caught? And so what? Watch me now. Sneakers hit the ground. Pink socks. Yellow shorts. White shirt with bananas across it. Skin very pale and silk. Sunlight all over the girls' faces. The bra first. Like balls of sunlight, like the essence of summer and Peter cannot breathe now. It's just as he imagined, a soft nesting place like a secret cave, and the two girls wild with summer lean into the water and each other.

Drowning

the holy water in the stained glass window forgotten
flies drank it by day by night bacteria grew
the woman in blue found a bee drowning in it
poured the water on a plant the bee was dead

yesterday's mail had a letter from an old lover
saying her cat had died the one she left
with him in Tucson fourteen years ago
she tried to remember the cat named Loan Shark

what did it look like? now dead in a house fire
where her her ex-lover lived in Wyoming
but is driving the cat's body back across state lines
for a proper burial in Arizona

pour out the cat's body in a nearby grave she thinks
the cat had a black face and white chin she remembers
her ex lover was very thin when they parted
she cannot remember his face now

Hotel Room, Patterns of Light

And now you whose face I have nearly forgotten
Remember how you said you would change the world?
Remember how you smoked weed and drank tea and told me
in one hotel room after another how glad you were
you knew your purpose?
Remember how you painted me a picture on birch bark,
a canoe paddling upstream carrying light in the stern?
As if one canoe could make a difference.

Remember how you went to Flagstaff to visit your mother?
When you came back you said, I slept with this hooker
over the holiday, Sweetness, had to see what it was like
to order a woman around.
I remember the pattern of light on the hallway floor
shadowed with these little slivers of darkness
that kept disappearing. I opened and closed my mouth
several times without speaking. Like a fish I was.

Before I left, I dropped the birch bark on the floor.
You left it there, sat rocking back and forth.
Don't go, you said. But you looked all hollow to me.
I could see the door right through you.
Your voice sounded faraway, like a radio station
you can never tune in. I walked out into the cold air,
open sunlight. Last I heard you were in furniture sales.
Measuring success one couch at a time.

Coffee and Cigarettes

Coffee reminds me of cigarettes,
which I never smoked,
but the smell used to cover my skin
in bars with lights flashing,
a great mirrored ball that caught
each glistening palm held out, each desperate face.
There were two kinds.
Those there for fun.
Those there to quench loneliness.
Find a mate. I was for fun.

Didn't care about mates or mating,
just the hot lights on my bare shoulders and midriff,
the feet of dancers going faster and faster
while the eternally banal music,
hopped, rumbled, vibrated, slithered.
I danced with whoever would dance with me.
I'd crawl back to bed exhausted.
Wake smelling of cigarettes,
on my hair, clothes, bed sheets.
Spend half of Sunday cleansing.

The lonely men and lonely women smelled different.
They smoked, drank bourbon sloppily.
Their mouths too wide and greedy like sharks or anacondas.
They would shake your hand and hold on.
The hand kept them from shaking out of control,
collapsing in a dizzy spin on the dance room floor.
But loneliness is in the eyes. Dreadfully hollow,
like the eye sockets of a skull.
Sockets that cry out for moisture
from any passing living thing.

The men, if they find a victim, will wake beside her
hands empty, heart floor bare. Will wait for another night,
another bar, another drink of woman.
The women are far more dangerous.
They will suck in their victim for life if they can.
They have hooks and chains: Children, the promise of sex
that will be free and easy and nightly.
It will cost mortgages, dresses, dinners, movies,
vacations to foreign counties, remote islands, hammocks,
jewelry, a free ride on the lifelong hormone roller coaster.

He'll tell himself it's fun.
It's life. It's marriage.
It's what I was born for.
Eating lies like rice for sustenance.
In another country, rice is all they have.

In another life, light endlessly moved.
The air was thick with bourbon and cigarettes
Prince Charming was waiting to be found
True love was out there
in that giggling crowd on the dance floor.

I was having the time of my life
escaping from nothing
and to nothing.
In the morning I stank.
The smell of coffee reminds me now.

Brewer

To escape the bears of winter,
he went south
filled his glass with soft amber liquid,
sat back, took a drink, smiled.

A woman crawled into his lap
asking for more than she gave
swallowing his lips like so many oysters,
webbing in his arms like a silk worm.

The light changes rapidly.
A police flashlight shines in his eyes
and that question from high above him,
where are you going?

He's been asking himself that for many years,
and now this jerk in uniform
thinks he's going to spit our
the answer of the ages through fuzzy lips?

I'm on a powerful journey,
he tells the cop,
and this woman's going with me
to discover her purpose in life.

The woman's face is all shadows and loose hair.
She clutches amber to her throat.
Her words arrive late and jumbled
like a cold fish from a reluctant waiter.

The cop waves the man on his journey;
the man lifts up his hands to bless the cop.
He blesses the shadows drifting down the sidewalk,
the passerby, the old city below sea level.

In his room alone, he turns on a porn channel
and begins to dance,
slowly, fumble-footed at first,
then a tango, finally a waltz.

Mating Season

We fight. It's hot. It's rangy. It's humid.
We're out of money. Can't afford sushi.
Can't afford Chinese food. Your mother's crazy.
My mother's a saint, and you can't see it.
You started working out Tuesday, described the teacher's
breasts when you got home.
After a couple shots.
That'll help your workout.
We fight. I say I'll kick that teacher
next time we meet.
You say, aha.
Fuck you in the blue and black twilight.
In the deepening thick air as night creeps
up on us in our street and dirt,
claims the crab grass yard.
We're sitting outside
with our glasses watching for stars
can't see much but smog and dirty light,
like the light worms see from under a thin layer of soil.
You say, back in Canada it's time for spring planting,
time to plow. Ah, I think, mating season.
We go in then, lock the door.
No stars. No moon.
Just tangled confusion.
Smell of wine and incense.
Sorrow.
Anxiety.
Pain.
Hormones.
Love even.
Maybe love.
Mating season,
I say. Here goes.

Demanding Barbados

The sky, yellow over the city of faded silks,
flat booze, cigarette smell on every glass.
Dying men under freeways. You drive.

You aren't sure why the city reminds you of a painting
or what painting you'd like to be inside of.
It's an orange hat the girl's wearing that reminds you of death.
The leaves gone from this part of the world.

The girl next to you wears perfume. She is close enough,
you can see the layers of makeup, the body work,
necessary for this beauty. In the restaurant you stare
at a man outside with a stick of dynamite in his hand.

For dynamite, you are ready. For the perfumed woman,
you are not sure. The yellow light of the city
is all around you. You can go to sleep. You can wake up.
Nothing will change.

If you dream of eagles, it will only distract you
from your purpose in the hive. You are part of
the buzz of yellow wings. The city has eaten you
and Julia. You walk woodenly as if your skin were very dry.

The man with dynamite is ready now. The woman leans toward you
whispering. You feel her rock hard breasts against your arm. Imagine
those hands pouring wine for you, that throaty voice laughing and
laughing, demanding Barbados.

Crab Cake Special

And the light. The opaque equatorial light. The bush and the sea do not reflect the light but absorb it, suck it in, then glow morbidly.

                —Joan Didion

You are a woman.
You are a norteamericana.
You drive to the hotel
with blue roofs by the sea.
The clouds move slowly.
The pool is shiny. Pain
vanishes under the shimmery surface
of all that ocean,
all those glittering waves.
The piles of sky are unbearable.

The smell of ocean is too much for sleep
which is what you crave.
You came here to rest.
You will never drive up to the gates
of your gated community
the same, now that you've had time
to rest and reflect and refresh
your tan and soul.
Really, this weekend is what you needed.
All is well. All is well.

Orange roughy tonight? Is a pale fish.
Best with white or a sparkling wine.
You prefer red moony wines that
fall flat into your system
taking up the space that glows
reaching beyond mapped territories,
longitudunal equatorial currents.
Unchartered oceans deep in your watery
self are where red wine reaches.
All is well, and then—chop chop—noise—

Some stupid movie about Argentina.
Stop it, turn it off.
Have a drink.
Dinner tomorrow night in the restaurant
with the tiny red booths.
Crab cake special.
God, those homeless people.
You want to do something.
It's too much.
You can't even solve your own.

You prefer a light broth
with the crab cake special
and that wonderful bread
prepared in the bakery next door.
You can smell yeast rising.
Your face dips into your hands
but comes up, still a face
still empty of divinity.
Dead things everywhere
and you without magic.

Newton's Bar

My drunken brother staring boorish at the curtains
yellow and hanging silky, sheer-like crescents of the moon
where you can see blackness through.

Waitress comes by. Deep throated gal. Leans over my brother
her front spilling forth. Looked good to me.
If you were a crazy Chinamen's teacup, you'd catch some.

Ah, you'd guzzy up and lip some. You'd gobble eye-fulls
and trade your fingers for extra hands,
fist fulls. Candy.

But not brother. He looked at the woman like you'd look
at rotting meat or a dead porcupine hanging on a squash vine
in hot summer. Dull buzzard stare.

My brother says he's all for women's rights. Hates pornography.
It's the women themselves that make him taste bile in his teeth.
A flash of leg, a curve, wet lips, flat belly, their bodies.

All that shining he detests.
And their smell, that everlasting smell, reminds him of his
mother. We have different mothers. Mine smelled like comfrey.

Don't get fresh with me, this waitress says, and I can see
she's angry. Unused to being despised. The kind of woman
who thinks males want a breath or taste.

My brother wanted to go home then.
Have a little orgy with the streets wretched-like,
a little vomiting maybe if the booze wouldn't stay down.

Going home he insisted I drive faster, running over squealing
things on the way. He sang out the window.
Songs about himself, screaming, Faster, brother, faster.

His head hit a bat. His laugh was huge in the night air.
The bat is neither mouse nor bird. It lived to fly away,
procreate, make more of its indefinable species.

My brother's shape against the night air haunts me still.

Lilac Season in Catalina

The man with the boat called *Lilac Season* fell flat on his face on the plank
wood floor of a Catalina bar. His girlfriend leaned over, her breasts the first
things he saw when he opened his eyes. Her friend, a topless dancer from
Phoenix, apologized to the crowd for lack of class, said she had hoped to make
a good impression on the good people of Catalina. Ms. Lilac Time cried out
that she had no money and ordered Miss Topless to buy her another Bufffalo
Milk. The sunlight was heavy, the air full of ocean and boat gasoline.
Ms. Lilac Time swigged her drink and ordered her husband a tall beer. Miss
Topless held the old man, his hands travelling the decks, and Ms. Lilac Time
was ready to fight for the old fellow with his red rimmed eyes. She had her
silicon, her blond hair, her unravelling mind, and her full prescription of Prozac.
Fuck you Miss Topless. I can smile too. Watch me smile. Watch me hold him
on the dance floor. Watch me, with such grace I dance darling. At forty, can
you do this? Can you hold a fucked-up man in your arms and smile and dance?

Blue Heron, Chaos

Mother's down again. She drinks after four o'clock. She's an equal opportunity drinker. Beer, wine, fuzzy navels, tequila on the rocks, sake, Coors Light (she's on a diet!), an imported dandelion beer you can only get in specialty stores. Lightly Jack, lightly, salt the rim, sip it gently, ghostly sweet, Jack sweet love of my life, Jack, it's take-out food again for dinner, let's dance, come on baby, some music baby, watch Mama dance.

When she slumped to the couch, me and Jack'd drink down the remains. Me and Jack'd raid the fridge. Me and Jack'd smoke the cigs. Me and Jack'd smoke the weed. Me and Jack'd climb to Mama's bedroom. Me and Jack'd pretend to be Daddy and his pals in the pen. Me and Jack is half brothers see. Me and Jack used to practice bringing in Mama's head on platter to Dad and he'd be so pleased. My, we'd tickle his fancy with that. Now Daddy's in the pen, me and Jack polish Daddy's shotgun.

When my hand got blowed off, me and Jack were just pussyfooting around and we seen this blue heron out the back, and we said, let's shoot him, and we pull the trigger, and then this goddam' noise and blackness, and even Mamma come to, and I hear her say, "chaos" before it's all ringing down, all the bells, and I'm thinking I see chariots come to get me. I think I see them lights and chariots and hear them bells.

Mama was drinking about four that afternoon; it was grasshoppers, Mama was singing too, swing low, early in the afternoon before Jack and me see that blue heron.

Jagged Pieces of Language

See that kite, honey? Life's like that.
You stringing along, nobody really watching.
The air very cold. Talk to God, plum cake.
It planned this.
It on its cold, rosy throne.
Throwing out jagged pieces of language.

Let there be this.
Let there be that.
Raising its dark hands.
Batter my heart, three-personed God, somebody asked.
Well, the average human gets that wish.
Gets battered.

The clouds hanging overhead,
laugh at you, stringing along.
Like an explosion.
A lightning storm would amuse.
You will be cold.
You will be hot.

The air will taste salty or wet.
Or grimy as the case may be.
You will see blue.
The earth will move violently.
You will feel air and water rushing.
The way to control your flight is not to control it.

Only Calvinists believe that.
We aren't kites on a string.
Far from it.
Kites have their own little souls,
held in the cup of someone's hand
while the kite is bucked about.

We are dreamers so dreams dream us.
Nothing happens we didn't design.
Give God a tall order.
Ask for a baby, a lover a million bucks.
Mon Dieu est si grand, si fort et si puissant.
It won't hear a thing you say.

It's doing its funky hair in its funky sky
while you're praying. It's doing fujimama.
You will pray at some time in your life.
Then you'll make something happen.
Or you won't.
If you do, you'll tell yourself God did it.

It will do the fujimama some more, so go figure.
It's about as interested in your little life as smog is.
You want to change your life?
Prayer wouldn't be the first best step.
You'll find creative dreaming goes further
than blue nights praying.

Downwind of you someone is helplessly leaning into the stars
whispering, I am a kite and it isn't my fault.
Katydid dreamed that once.
Nothing good ever happened by dreaming
except for Martin Luther King in Alabama
or Ghandi.

Nothing else.
Much.
Ever.
You will carry your soul around in a small twisted
paper bag asking God every day how to change it
into a swan, a dirty bird, but you don't know that.

God will have Its hair done up in dreadlocks.
The world was without form and void.
Darkness was upon the face of the deep.
God said, Let there be light.
Light feels like a whack in the head some mornings,
especially if you're hung over.

The crowded places in our minds where dreams hang out.
Transformation dreams get eaten by.
Soup crackers cops sirens radio freeways appointments.
Transformation dreams get eaten by.
Yellow-bellied bomb freaks people with expensive hair
guys asking for gas money to spend on a smoke.

I am not a box kite myself. I'm a rainbow dragon kite
with a long tail. When the wind stops, I fly along
on my own power pausing now and then to change direction
or to pray for wind or light. If the wind doesn't come,
I say, Let there be wind. Or light. Whichever I want first.
Kites flying loosely screaming out the name of God.

Blue Russians

As soon as my husband rose from his chair by the fire, my son took his place and pushed his cold feet in my lap. I rubbed them absently with my sleeve, continued to read. You are not related to him, my son says, do you know that? You are related to me and my sister and to your parents if you have them and to your grandparents.

But I have no parents or grandparents. As I said, he says, my point exactly. And why is everyone so mean to me? Look at him, having so much fun, the time of his life. He points across the lake to my husband with his son, the green trees behind them glowing. My sister playing in the lake, and you're mean and reading, and I say, Ah, so.

The lake fairly shimmers with color and frogs. The sky is blue Russians juggling white clouds like plates and saucers. My son grimly puts on his sneakers. No one's listening, he says. What am I supposed to do? Make the world? and I keep smiling and point out a duckling that's starting feathers already.

Marriage to an Artist

*I've eaten a lot of grilled onions, I've also spent a long time
calling myself a creative person, an artist. Believe me, any-
one who says that of herself is saying, 'I know how to make
everything except a decent living.'*
                                    —Annie La Ganga

Sculpt away, she says.
Who do you think you are? Rodin?
He'd left a thriving dental practice
for cloudy objects he shaped in oddly mixed colors.
He thrives on cruel invectives
from former colleagues,
weighs them against the pleasure
of calling himself an artist.

She now has two jobs, limited toilet paper.
They sell the antiques and stereo.
She buys a songbird, whistles more often.
Money isn't important, he says, ignoring the answering machine.
Money clouds your judgement and impairs true feeling
Don't you realize art is everything?
Bring home a six pack of beer.
I'm working on a sculpture of Chloe all night.

I have to sleep and get up in the morning, she says,
sorry for the lack of inventive structure in my life,
but due to a couple of bad judgement calls on my part,
one in particular that I don't want to discuss at the present
because I might hit someone,
I'm plumb out of creative space right now.
Rodin was a genius, he says.
I know, she says, but I'm only interested in unsung heroes.

Have it all your own way, you always do.
I will, she says, I do.
When you're on the retreat next weekend,
I'll get things hammered out.
You do that.
I will, she says.
I'll get it all hammered out,
and things will be back to normal.

Happily Ever After

Blouses opening rain.
Hot plans crashing.
Eye glasses needed.
Blood eyes winter.
Come on, now.
Lips cracked winter.
That's all darling.
You go now.
Yellow fast places.
Red under places.
He's been there.
She's blue alone.
Countertops linoleum cleaning.
All that's left.
Black fissured nothing.
Ugly crows landing.
Long black skirts.
Filling the sidewalks.
Remember ring gold.
Marry me please.
I want up.
Don't hit me.
Yes I'll cook.
I'll good you.
I'm tongue ready.
Blood under nails.
Nothing bothers me.
Leaving walking away.
Come one now.
Clouds then rain.
You haven't been.
Anywhere I've been.
Caves of thought.
Blistering silence cold.

The new approach.
Walk up behind.
Hide your stick.
Ask first, please.
Kiss the fingers.
That's always nice.
Then say softly.
Have we met?
She'll say, no.
She'll look wicked.
She'll look everywhere.
Not at you.
Ignore this, try.
Say, I wish
I'd known you.
Say, I'd like
to know you.
Say, I'm looking
for someone, you.
Say, you're beautiful.
I'll give you
everything and anything.
She'll stare back.
Her eyes empty
as light sockets
a grinning skull,
her face bright
with imitation smile.
White teeth gleam
face glimmers pale.
Go away now.
You twisted, fucker.
Her legs scissors.
Opening and closing.

Egg shell mine.
Silence mine always.
My thoughts tapping
windowpane madness tap.
You knew it.
The caves everything.
Come on, now.
I'm dreaming you.
You're someplace else.
Perhaps it's better.
Watch romantic movies.
Imagine the ending.
Kids with me.
Sloppy nights breathing
I can't sleep.
Wish another life.
No fixing yours.
Happily ever after.

Die. Die. Die.
You without language.
Women are dealers.
They smile. Smile.
You turn away.
Another woman, maybe.
Again, maybe not.
Go to sleep.
No more fantasy.
Hit the lights.
Kill the porn.
Video's not helping.
Reality is you
are all alone
night after night
you tell yourself
you're better off
now she's gone.

Daughter

Learn how to fight. Learn how to fight back. Don't let anyone hit you. Don't let anyone hurt you. Learn how to get away. Learn how to get away quickly. Learn how to leave in the middle of the night. Learn how to leave while he is sleeping. Learn how to take care of yourself. Learn how to take care of your children. Learn how to take care of your brother. Learn how to run. Learn how to look over your shoulder. Learn how to run in the dark. Learn how to swim. Learn how to ride a wild horse. Learn how to sail. Learn how to sail away. Learn how to make your own money. Learn how to save your own money. You will be careful. You will remember all I told you, won't you?

Son

Be nice to women. Be nice even if they aren't pretty. Even if they are fat, ugly or stupid. Be nice. They will not be nice to you. They will say unkind things behind your back. They will take your money. They will lure you into bed. They will get pregnant. They will marry you. They will have your children. They will take your money. They will fall asleep when you want to make love. They will ask you for things. You will give them things. The children will ask you for things. You will be the giver of things and money. They will talk about you with other women. You will be careful. You will be nice, won't you?

Foreign Objects so Close to Home

blood around the edges of the green bathrobe
and on the door knob
he leaves

for the weekend
time enough for her to clean up
she retreats to her vodka and music

he travels with a briefcase swinging
like a fist
his breath heavy

this will be the last time he thinks
they can't go on like this
he hears himself cursing in his sleep

his own voice waking him
fucking whore slutbitch
he sees the stain on the wall

below the picture of her on her first horse
her face breaking into a smile
what world has he stumbled into here

he stares at his own hands
they are foreign objects
so close to home

He holds her for a moment
rocking and whispering
her hair stinks

there is a bottle on the counter
he could break it
and tenderly reach

for the wonder
that was this woman
when he found her

but this is not the last bottle
there's another
a line of bottles

going back to casks and vats
and gourds to the first grape
from the first garden

turning potent
into a thousand screaming days
a thousand blood soaked nights

Direct Action

The eucalyptus trees have loose bark
a tangle of branches
Light shifts noiselessly on the dusty bank
The trees move in the wind
The air is hot, thin, dangerous
Buddy slaps down his orange hat by the freeway
All those cars going to the ocean
Last night his wife did not speak to him
or move from the couch
Her face hard in the blue light
moths flew into the screen over and over
He heated the rice
His wife wore a green bathrobe
When he spoke to her she grunted
The air sizzles
He leans toward the eucalyptus tree
You first he says snapping the match
The sky way too blue
The people on the freeway
too satisfied rich and cozy in their cars
He will change all that.
He sees the first flame reaching out for the next.

Necessary Solitude

We are unable to separate
dead leaves from an elm tree
if we let ourselves get confused enough.

Finally, we're cooking fish in olive oil with red pepper
and we start to think that the poems
we've been sitting with aren't really poems at all.

They're cows marching into the dairy to be milked
and pretty soon, if it goes on like this,
we can't tell solitude from trousers.

Unless the heart is left alone,
it cannot distinguish between itself and your pantry
all spider webs and canned goods.

Baby Powder

Sometimes the door is open a crack
and Johnson looks out
at the dimly lit apartment hallway
and asks Ruby to get some cigarettes.

Sometimes Ruby goes downstairs to get them.
Sometimes she leaves the door standing open
so Johnson has to close it. And ever after
the baby is born, Johnson never leaves.

Disability check arrives. Mornings. Rain.
Baby cries. And he's the perfect sitter, Ruby says.
Cause he ain't going nowhere
and that baby growing up just like him .

She'll sit watching television with him for hours
eating them Vienna sausages right out the can,
and frozen waffles they'll toast up weekends just for something
special with jelly on 'em and peanut butter sometimes.

Oh Johnson can cook all right. When tips is good,
he'll fry up a steak as rare as you please.
With a little salt and ketchup.
You can't beat it with a stick.

Course that baby's blind all right.
Blind as a newborn terrier, blind as a baby rat.
His fault, Ruby says. But that baby's keeping him happy,
she says. More or less. He stays on that couch mostly.

I ain't never talked to him about the accident.
I was drunk and it was hard getting him into
the driver's seat. He never talks about it.
I don't talk to him none either.

Pillar of Salt

I'm in trouble, she says,
but he isn't listening.
I'm turning into salt.

She would remember, the soft whirring air,
while the heat blazed along behind them.
My wife left me, was how he put it.

She wouldn't follow simple orders.
and I moved in with my daughters,
I needed someone to take care of me.

His wife dropped his things into the fire one by one.
Glass ice, she says, formed all around me. I broke
out of my skin, formed a wall around myself in lieu of singing.

He doesn't remember her hands stretched out.
He doesn't remember her at all.

Modele

Trust me, he said
and pulled off her gloves.
We can be friends.
One shoe. Close friends.
Then the other.
He buried his face in her feet
and ejaculated in the arches.
She slipped sideways
as she entered the bathroom.
Climb out the window, he said.
Before my wife gets home.
Nothing's stopping you.
I'll clean up here.
And by the way, you're the one
who got me into this.
She got out on the ledge.
From up there she could see the wife
unpacking the groceries,
entering the front door.
Got your favorite soup,
she sang, and the olives and cheese
you like, and the bread.
I spent oodles on champagne
so we can bubbly tonight.
The woman on the ledge leans
down to hear his reply.
A scrap of red coat catches his eye.
Be back in a minute, he says
and steps outside.
Get going! He whispers.
You'll be the death of me!
The woman drops lightly onto the snow
and disappears in the fading light.
He pauses, then calls, Come back.

But she is already gone.
Inside his wife asks, who were you talking to?
I saw you gesturing with your arms.

He stares at her as if she is unrecognizable.
For a moment, I believed there was something solid
out there, but the light tricked me and it was gone.

Shattering Blind Windows

Well try it on, honey, let's see.
Now there, you're beautiful. Look at yourself.
I can't believe you've grown so much.
All those softball summers and soccer winters

when I waited for you to grow
so your father and I could start living.
Me? I'll just poke around here.
We have all day. Can stay till evening.

She stares in the mirror while her daughter dresses.
Treacherous travel. The waiting years over.
The weight of children vaporizing.
The weight of nothing descending.

She watched the filling of a man-made lake in Canada once.
The tree stumps and rocks suddenly submerged.
Water rushing in. Knowing all those possible
branches and trees would vanish forever.

Stumps, homes for insects. Gone.
Not even a diver to go down deep with a flashlight
and report back. A young pine feels wind and sunlight
for the last time before water arcs and shudders over it.

In the end, sunlight on leaves, wind, firestorms, will be a story
they will tell. A story listeners half believe.
The reality dark, murky
water-sogged and completely dead.

Goldenrod

The fields were that full of goldenrod that when you sniffed, it smelled hot
and honey, like air woven with pollen and when you got home, Mama was
slapping down fish into a pan of frying oil singing, "Oh baby, don't you weep,
don't you mourn, Pharoah's army got drowned," and the sunlight shined over
her so she squinted and looked pleased to see you for once but stopped to hit
you anyway. It was that sort of day, and the pain didn't last long. You crawled
under the stairs, found a piece of chewed gum, you'd left for later. Ah it was
that kind of day, smell of garlic under the stairs. Everything perfect.

The Prisoner's Wings

I draw a sky map for my husband
who is in prison by the coast to show him
how to escape by sea using celestial navigation.
Use the stars as your guide.
Travel by night. Don't use freeways.
The prison he stays in is
forty-four floors high.
His cell the eighty-ninth in its row.
He wears a special uniform,
does certain repetitive tasks every day
during which he is permitted to sing
the national anthem and gospel songs.

My instructions guide him to escape
from his cell through the maze
to a certain open window.
The thing he has to do is build wings.
The wings are eleven feet long
and built entirely of light particles.
They have the effect of drowning out darkness.
Even after they are built,
he is afraid to use them,
confused about where to go when he lands.
I say, who cares where you land?
Just get out of the building.

My husband's mother praises my efforts
on her son's behalf, but she liked to point
out that someone needs to stay in the cells,
that if everyone escapes, we'd have chaos,
feathers, wings everywhere,
way too many non-uniformed personnel.
Her favorite quote is, No hive, no honey.
I write to my husband, send the message by starlight,
two words, Wild honey. Next day he puts on his wings.
Sky map in hand, he is ready.
Dear me, his mother keeps saying, shading her eyes,
will those wings really hold him?

Mulholland Drive

From up there the Valley and City are pretty.
In photographs, she's pretty, he's pretty.
They're usually on vacation somewhere pretty.
He's touching her shoulder, and if it's night, she's staring
off someplace that matters as if she had night vision.

From the top of Mulholland Drive, you can pretend you're
someone else. You're one of the pretty people, somewhere
that isn't your crummy place with the trash cans out front.
The neighbors always talking some other language that
sounds happy and not at all like English.

The view from Mulholland Drive is like foreplay.
Always better than the actual act when you're close enough
to smell the wasted beer breath, feel the clammy hands.
You can't get away, can't drown yourself, too many lifeguards.
You'd like one of those lives, but they aren't easy to get.

They start with somebody seeing you and nobody's seen you yet.
Pretty people have visible forms. Other people are invisible.
You're invisible. You're in the dark over Mulholland Drive,
the lights winking and shining and laughing at you, remembering.
Remembering what?

Solomon's Problem

It's a ragged gesture of disappointment. I wish I'd unlaced her blouse once.
I wish I'd kissed him. Drunk as we were, it wouldn't have mattered. I wish
we'd frolicked last night in the damp air, his hair standing up in the heat,
mine shorn until the suffocating lilies were limp and crushed. I wish I'd
gotten up early to write, wish I'd planted irises at dusk. Painted the boxwood
tree in lamplight. It's staring at your teeth in the morning, our faces bleary
and stained. So much for Sinatra, Father would have said after a night of
dancing with whores mistresses or pretended nieces I still feel like hell in
the morning. I have all these regrets, so many women , not enough nights,
Solomon's problem, yours too . . . and he the wisest of men.

Tequila

I'm not asking you for anything.
You can ignore me.
You can just go on
living your life as if I don't exist.
You don't have to call me.
You don't have to visit at Christmas.

I'll mail your gifts.
I'll mail them to your stepmother's house.
That bitch that's sleeping with your father.
I have nothing against her,
or him either, the son of a bitch,
but he better remember who the real mother is.

You can take your little trips.
Don't worry about me, son. I'm fine.
I'm not asking you for anything.
I'm stuck here in this miserable hell hole,
and you know what I do?
I suck my fingers.

I stare across the way at Maria,
whose son comes over every day
to just water the roses
and have ice tea with her,
and they sit there and laugh.
That bitch does not know how lucky she is.

But as God is my witness, my son,
I'm not asking for anything.
You can live your life as you please.
You can keep taking your little trips
with that little tramp.
What is it you're drinking these days?

It used to be tequila.
I always keep a bottle on hand
so when you stop by, we can drink it down.
You can't live on air.
Remember how we used to laugh and drink?
Remember how we used to laugh?

Thursdays I Spend by the Window

The woman who eats raw ears of corn meets the man in their shared office. The clouds sever the sun from the basin of the room. The floor is full of shadows. He brings in a little coffee and a cream pitcher, offers her some. The cream is cold. She sips hers, finds it to her liking, eats an orange section by section, asks his name. David's eyes fly around the room as he delivers his name on a high note of expectancy, knowing she'll forget it as soon as she retreats to the crawlspace of her mind. David waits. Brings in cranberries and caviar, shoelace black, asks her to stop by after work. Tells her about the disease. Tells her while his hands shake. Useful. Elicits pity. Hopefully pity. Not contempt. Never contempt, Elise feels. Curiosity. Animal curiosity. Drives to his place around the corner from the store that sells chainsaws over by Fifth. Near the water. Brings melons sliced and pomegranates whole. Oh yes. He has wine ready. Wants to chat. Just that. A friend. Sit down, why don't you? Play the piano. You can hear the ocean. See the sun sliding down. She is by the window. He is in his chair drink in hand. She says, Don't move. If you get up from that chair, I leave. You understand? and he says, Yes, and I'll be a good boy, though he's nearly fifty, and, I'll do whatever you say. So, she says. It's your birthday. Though she's making that up. Here's a little treat for you. Something to remember me by. She undresses slowly, standing by the window, silk underwear last, striptease slow. She turns several times, then stands with her back to him for a few seconds before putting on one article at a time. How was that? she says, and he says, Better than carrot juice, and she laughs. Thursdays? and he says, I don't mind. She turns back to the window. The twilight had begun while she was naked. It is all around them now.

The Boxer

Punching and jabbing that bag every day, Henry's muscles like heavy cord, his brain a round pounding place. Liza spills the plate of spaghetti and he turns around, quick as a cat, fist raised and swinging.

Liza's lover says he saw her the next morning at breakfast. That they ate at the corner cafe, grits and toast with marmalade.
But there's lots who say what with the weed and the random pussy he was pummelling, how can he be sure of the day he saw Eliza?

Henry shaves his head, sprinkles sawdust in the kitchen. He eats his raw burger makes love to his punching bag. Liza wasn't much of a cook anyway, but it was too bad about the baby. Was going to be a little boxer named Joey. Was going to make his dad proud. Too bad Liza had to louse things up.

Dominoes

I am not amused. I am not easily amused. Other people are amused, sometimes lightly amused, sometimes frothy with laughter like a banana shake. I am still as rancid pond water covered with beetle dung. I am tracing the trail of my own stillness back to my mother telling my father, All right you can to it to me, but I don't want you to. You can do it to me, but I'd rather be doing anything else right now. I'd rather do push-ups on the floor or situps on the bench or read my Bible in the rocking chair or cook some potatoes than lie here on the bed my legs apart, you poking and prodding and then with a jerk and thrust your hands gripping air, it's all a convulsion of thick breathing and that swift gulp on my part of leftover air and then that sweet sticky smell and that's over. If we've conceived another child, I'm telling you I'll kill myself. Baby too. You love the dog, he said. Toto too. But gutless never followed through. Waited till I was out of diapers to give me away. Kept the dog. Years of suffocation and closets and beatings later I see it in living color and I want to call up. If I had the number. If she had a phone. If any cord still connected us. I'd say Dorothy got Toto. That's the way the story goes. But now out into the plain of semi-thinking people with desires for little lives of consuming small cheeses and rinky dink cars and monstrous kitchen appliances. The god of malls demands a sacrifice. It's just not very amusing to me. Whole shards of splintered cranium are what I deal with mostly and creation of self or even some magic lettered ball. I invited god over for dinner to talk about wrestling. She helped me rub the chicken with paprika and lemon. We agreed on a wine. We ate rice. She told me her grandson plays the blues in a tavern over on Fourth Street We played dominoes into the night. Black, and white falling over and over in little heaps. That's god. Not angry over small things. Not worried about stupid people. Just amused. Telling me about the fair and riding the ferris wheel. Up and down and creating light magic while the big wheel spins. I'm not easily amused I said over our fourth game. Gently, she said, gently, you're not as special as you think you are. And you're infinitely more the only dandelion like you than you ever imagined. Follow the rain trails and star maps back to where they started making things up; you'll see how that's done, see where birdsong comes from. And where's the hot chocolate? Ever sweet. On the tongue. Ever longing. The toast, my darling, with marmalade. Ever rich in dreamswim.

What Jamie Saw

In the classroom full of yellow walls, she seemed very cold
wrapped in silence, the veins on her wrists
were light blue and quite visible in that glaring light.
Her ears protruded slightly, a hat at a rakish angle
slow smooth eyebrows slanting up when the teacher spoke.

I saw her every day wearing the same brown coat,
a red lace muffler like something a Spanish matron would wear.
Over all, an air of sadness and hope
so I followed her home to study, I said
and she nodded without asking questions.

I wanted to see the inside of her face which I hoped
would be reflected in the house. That it wouldn't be
a shining teacup of a place lit and polished
in her father's colors and her mother's taste. Holding light
like one of those snow globes, all pre-made and ready-to-order.

It was one card table and the smell of pickles,
an electric typewriter, two spoons on the counter
a cat asleep on the floor, a stack of books in the corner,
a picture on the wall of Van Gogh's sunflowers
cut from the newspaper,

one big pink lamp with "garage sale" written all over it.
She wrestled with her coat, got it off,
offered me hot tea, which I drank carefully
wishing for my classroom girl, wishing
to back out of this small meanness

hating to see her wearing trousers, that green sweater,
sitting so small on the mustard-colored carpet. She'd started
a plant on the windowsill fragile green tendrils.
The box that held her few clothes was the one
the typewriter came in. It said, "Open here, handle with care."

Lunar Contamination

Unwind your eyes
I told the young fellow
what you need is just slices of air
He'd slapped me full-face on the way to breakfast
I sliced my green melon
cool and ripe

A younger me would have laughed at his insolence
and forgotten him like yesterday's leaves.
I want to know what an older me would do
his teeth shine
as he turns the heel of his palm
as a greeting

this older me would hold
this boy's face and gestures
like a basket of moon bread,
wondrous strange sticky stuff
which must be disposed of properly
to avoid contamination

Moon bread tingles in the hands
if held too long without protection.
This mother's face is ghost pale
in the unearthly lunar glow.
With no masks, no gloves, no proper equipment
for handling wet fissuring danger.

The Night I Saw Jesus

I met Jesus in disguise at a bar one evening. I recognized him and asked if he'd like to buy me a drink. He shook his head, so I bought myself a screwdriver and gave him my phone number. He just shoved his cowboy hat down over his head and sipped a long necked Budweiser. The Holiday Inn in Pasadena was an odd place to run into the Son of God, but there was no doubt it was he. I asked the whereabouts of the Heavenly Father and whether or not he's ever said Hail Marys or did he have a cell phone connecting him directly to the throne room and if so what service did he use. Jesus ate some pretzels and slipped off his barstool onto the floor. I was right by his side when those policemen carried him out.

Ecstasy

A42 hadn't been at work long
when she needed the restroom.
She found her face with both hands
empty as a platter. "A42," the voice said,
"Return to work."
A42 turned her head sideways.
The walls were yellow.
The floors, sink, ceiling, toilets, all yellow.

A42 washed the corridors 96-115 every day
and returned to 19,642 where she had everything!
Television, bathtub, sex-a-whirl, ecstasy, rum, and
the orange pineapple flavored food she loved so much.
Sometimes A62 comes over to share.
They laughed and laughed at the television.
It's all so clever and brilliant, yet sad at the same time.
It's the sadness that touches A42.

A62 says life can't all be perfect. When they see the others,
they tell of the good times they've been having and
the things they've been laughing about. When A42 has a party,
they all come over to her level, and it's agreed afterward
that it was a pretty good time. On the television a spectacular
sunset over a perfect ocean wraps it up. Sometime,
they agree, they'll go to a beach resort and swim in a pool and
have ecstasy and rum with a sunset just like this one.

Winter Melon

Winter melon scrapes
the inside of her mouth
all blown back
green and ugly.
The child asks for more.
She doesn't notice or pretends not to
the tears filling.
Blow away candle fire.
I am inward turning on a spike.
My own loves entwine me. For what?
I can't tell anyone.
The blouse is mended now.
Roar, constable as loud as you like.
I shan't change a thing.
I'm enclosed in my own egg.
The dogs are barking madly.
while the general scratches
out demands for more weapons, more men.
An old man lives at the freeway underpass.
If you don't listen carefully,
you can't hear the ticking.
The moon is full, but no one in the city
sees it. People outside the city
only count as so many shards of clouds
racing across the summer night sky
blown back soon.
Still the orders keep coming while the trees fall.
There are always orders for more weapons.
While the orders are filled, we find ourselves dancing.
There's not much else to do.
In the city, people fall or jump from tall buildings
like leaves down they come
coating the sidewalks lying in pools of blood.
Cars race by. Heartache whispers at dusk.

Little lives flutter like church pigeons in the eaves
multiple, dirty, uncounted. It's not all crosses and holiness.
Mostly there are rows of coffins or mass graves
where the dead are all eyes.
The child can feel his mother's indifference,
closes his eyes with a sigh.
His word will have weight.
He'll sign his name in heavy black lettering
and the bishop will say, Amen.
The church is very quiet

while the bombs fall.
The child feels himself growing,
his core hardening, his mother becomes shadows.
He reaches for a knife, cuts the melon,
her hands open like birds' wings. They fly.

Sphere

You can't imagine the goats
who were my only friends as a child
how they tore at my underwear,
hitting their heads into my legs,
playfully throwing me into the air.
How their snores rattled the night.
How their milk tasted sweet
and thick and altogether wild.
How they followed me through the orchard
and up into the rocky fields above
and ate blueberries through the afternoon.
How at twilight I'd walk down,
a hand on two goats' backs
and they'd talk me all the way down.
How many times I was beaten
about the face and shoulders and back.
How the goat smell kept me
from properly experiencing food.
How I crept out to the goats in the night
and slept very well there
the goats licking my bruises as though I
were sacred and wounded and divine.

Biographical Note

Kate Gale received her Ph.D. in American Literature at Claremont Graduate University. She teaches English at Loyola Marymount University and California Institute of the Arts.

She is the author of six books. Four collections of poetry: *Blue Air, Where Crows and Men Collide, Selling the Hammock,* and *Fishers of Men*; a novel, *Lake of Fire* and a bilingual children's book, *African Sleeping Beauty*. She is the co-editor of four anthologies, *Anyone is Possible, Blue Cathedral, Fake City Syndrome,* and *The Crucifix is Down*.

Ms. Gale has had poems and short stories published in various literary magazines including *Arshile, Portland Review, Quarterly West,* and *The Connecticut Review* and has read at numerous venues including the Library of Congress. She was the first place recipient of the 1998 Allen Ginsberg Award. She is also a reviewer for the American Library Association's academic journal *Choice*.

She is the Managing Editor of Red Hen Press, a board member of PEN and the Editor of *The Los Angeles Review*. Her current project is *Rio de Sangre*, the libretto for an opera by Don Davis.